We Eat to Remember: Soul Food Poetry

BY FABU

THE IRONER'S PRESS

© 2023 Fabu Phillis Carter

ISBN: 978-1-949958-55-3 First Edition

Author's website: www.artistfabu.com

Published by: The Ironer's Press, 1102 Engleheart Drive, Madison, WI 53713

Cover photos: Sarah Karlson
Book design & graphics except as noted: Wendy Vardaman, wendyvardaman.com

All rights reserved. No part of this book may be reproduced, stored in whole or in part or transmitted in any form, by any means, without prior written permission from the author, except in the case of brief quotations included in articles for review. Nor can this book be circulated in any form of binding or cover other than that in which it is published.

This is an original, creative work. Any references or similarities to actual events, real people, living or dead, or to real localities are intended to give the poetry a sense of reality. Any similarity in other names, characters, places and incidents is entirely coincidental.

To all Black Farmers, especially to Grandaddy Woodie, Grandmama Effie & all their brothers and sisters who farmed and gardened in Holly Springs and Como, Mississippi

CONTENTS

SECTION ONE | AFRICAN FOOD: FREEDOM ORIGINS

Grace for the Nurturers | 2
African Eve | 3
Ummm Mmm Black Folks | 4
Our Food Story | 5
Traditional Cuisine | 6
Nguba | 7
Peppers from West Africa to America | 8
We Eat to Remember | 9
Sleep I am Free | 11
A Bowl Full of My Past | 13
This Strange Land | 14
Africa to America | 15
Dark Food for Dark People | 16
Caribbean Cuisine | 17
Tomatoes in Slave Times | 18
Watermelon Songs | 20
Our Food | 21
From the Fields and Waters | 22
The Whole Truth | 23
African to African American Cuisine | 24

SECTION TWO | SLAVERY: COOKING WITH LITTLE TO MAKE TASTY

Food and Freedom | 28
War and Famine in the New World | 29
Entering the New World | 30
Another Day a Slave | 31
God Will Call Us by Our Real Names | 32
Masters Are | 35
Poor Picaninny Gal | 36
Kamau Dies in the Cotton Patch | 38
How to Tell a Slaver | 39
Freedom is Food | 40

Corn and Pork | 41
Porky Pig | 42
Roastin Rabbit | 43
A Few Special Meals | 44
Another Hercules in Virginia | 45
Given to George Washington, 1767 | 46
George Washington, Slaveholder | 47
Another Hemings in Virginia | 48
Chef James Hemings | 49
Igbo Landing | 50

SECTION THREE | SOUL FOOD: AFRICA TO AMERICA

God, Love and Soul Food | 54
The Blues in Food | 55
Black Iron Skillets | 56
Grease Addiction | 57
Chow Chow | 58
We Cook with Little to Feed Many | 60
Head Hash | 61
A Tall Slim Bottle of Hot Sauce | 62
Dandelion Greens | 63
The Majesty of Greens | 64
Green Experts | 65
Potlikker | 67
Turnip Greens and Black Appetites | 68
A Marriage of Love | 69
For Carolina Rice | 70
A Brief History of Rice | 71
Hoppin John aka Black-Eyed Peas | 72
The Beginning of Us | 73
Okra Stories | 74
How to Eat Watermelon | 75
Watermelon Lyrics | 76

SECTION FOUR | MY HEALING GARDEN: COMO TO LIMURU TO MADISON

Gardens and Fabu | 80
The Patience of Seeds | 82
An Ode to Cukes | 83
Hot Peppers | 84
Green Cabbage Blues | 85
Eating Cabbage Leaves | 86
Collards Are Kings | 87
Soul Food Divas | 88
Mustards | 89
Okra Blooms | 90
Southern Okra | 91
Wild-in Out Tomatoes | 92
Bok Choy | 93
American Peas | 94
Lettuce Praise | 95
Modern Garden | 96
Badger Rock Community Garden | 97
Which Kind of Watermelon? | 98
Picking Sweet Melon | 99
You Better Grow | 100

SECTION FIVE | NOW WE EAT TO LIVE: LESS FAT, SALT, SUGAR AND RACISM

Creator of All Good | 104
Looking Back on Slavery | 105
Black Farmers Tribute | 107
Black Farmers and Nature | 108
Tribute to Soul Chefs | 109
Drinking Well Water | 110
Miss Annie's True Life Story | 111
Grandma Effie's Lopsided Cakes | 114
Grandma Effie's Scratch Biscuits | 115
Grandma Effie's Poke Salad | 116
Pink Happy | 117
Fried Corn Expert | 118

My Daddy Was a Cook Too | 119
Good Food During Pregnancy | 120
A Real Soul Food Diet | 121
Arriving Home to Dinner Smells | 122
My Favorite Memories of Childhood Dinners | 124
Como, Mississippi Melons | 125
Enjoying Eating Watermelon | 126
A Modern Day Food Tragedy Reversed | 127

AFRICAN FOOD: FREEDOM ORIGINS

NUMBER OF ENSLAVED AFRICANS FORCED TO EMBARK TO EUROPE OR THE AMERICAS BY REGION (1514–1866)

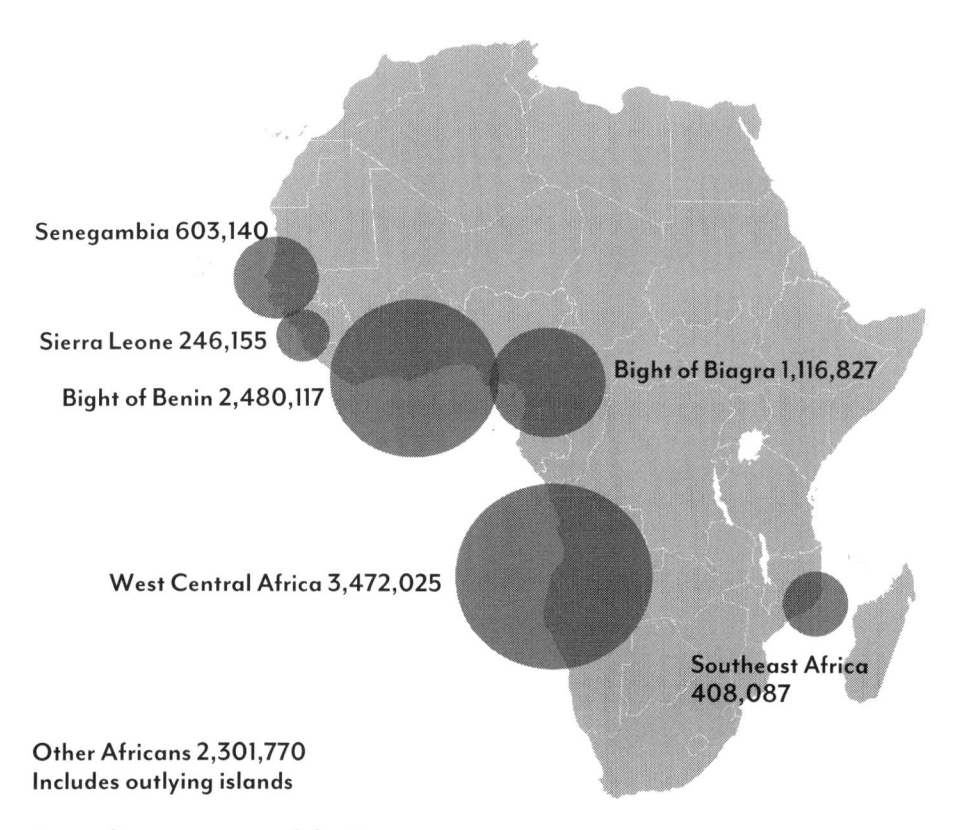

Senegambia 603,140

Sierra Leone 246,155

Bight of Benin 2,480,117

Bight of Biagra 1,116,827

West Central Africa 3,472,025

Southeast Africa 408,087

Other Africans 2,301,770
Includes outlying islands

Source: Slavevoyages.com & Statista

GRACE FOR THE NURTURERS

Grace prayed for nurturers
who bless the land
to produce well for us.

Grace prayed over those
who cultivate the soil
to hold good seeds they plant.

Grace prayed to the weeders
who pull up what should not be
to allow food to grow.

Grace prayed for the harvesters
Who gather God's bounty
to feed people everywhere.

AFRICAN EVE

Blackest
Thickest lips
Widest nose
Nappiest hair
Gal.

African
Imprinted
Atop Blackest skin
Across thickest lips
Woman.

Mitochondrial
Haplogroup Eve
Open nose
Curly hair
Ancestral Mother.

UMMM MMM BLACK FOLKS

Ummm mmm Black folks
Seeded full of spices
Planted in variations of Black
Producing colorful, flavorful fruit
If you want to engage all five senses
Love on Black folks.

Ummm mmm Black folks
Herbalicious
Skins like verdant leaves
Hibiscus flowers world-wide
Strong solid stems for garnishing
Love on Black folks.

OUR FOOD STORY

Our food is wrapped up inside vast stories
Of us as a complex people
Our stories didn't start in slavery so we go
Further back
To when all human histories started in Africa.

Traditional food is not fried or pork based
It is deep colored, plant based browns, greens,
Reds, and oranges
For our beans, peas, leafy greens, yams and fruits.

We used many spices to flavor
Cooking by roasting, steaming, boiling, pounding
We ate fruits and vegetables raw too.
Meals edged with Iru, Bitter Leaf, red, green and orange peppers
Sesame seed for everyday tastes.

Slavery meant little time to cook, eating leftovers scraps
Pork that massa didn't want; ears, tongue, guts,
Tails and feet that we made tasty
We free now and can eat what is best for our bodies
Spirits and minds.

Iru are West African fermented locust beans. Bitter Leaf, an indigenous African plant.

TRADITIONAL CUISINE

Our traditional cuisine teaches us
To cook slow and long.

Harvesting seasonal crops wisely
Drying and storing food carefully.

We pound herbs releasing
Flavors before boiling or roasting.

Plants and animals from the earth
Feed us and sustain our lives.

Loving the land and what it produces
Tastes best thru slow and low cooking.

All that changes during slavery
Fast and quick to cook and eat.

We fry plants and animal parts
Not for taste or health but for time.

We only have time to slave
In cotton fields, rice beds, tobacco rows.

We live quick and die quick
In a time where all is fast, including food.

NGUBA

Congolese for peanuts
Goobers
Groundnuts
Earthnuts
Ground peas
Southern name for peanuts.
An unknown African
Carried seeds in his pouch
Brought to America
Only eaten by poor folks,
Pigs and the hungry soldiers
In the Civil War.

PEPPERS FROM WEST AFRICA TO AMERICA

Africa is full of heat.
Peppers do more than fire food
with aromatic flavor.

Black pepper is well-tasted
Other peppers from spicy Africa
burn tongues.

Cayenne peppers are smaller
Chili peppers
flares 30,000 to 50,000.

Dry pepper
Ground *Piri piri* or chili
blazes from 50,000 to 175,000.

Ata rodo
Scotch bonnets
scorches from 80,000 to 400,000.

Tatashe
Bell peppers in red, yellow, orange
and green adds more color not heat.

No bland, plain, simple
spice for Black folks
peppers taste like our lives.

Tatashe is what Nigerians call bell peppers. *Ata rodo* is also known as Bonnet pepper or Caribbean red pepper.

WE EAT TO REMEMBER

African herbs and spices
enliven foods in our bellies
imprint on our memories
store strength in our DNA
while the tastes and smells
of everyday meals
are chained inside us
on the transatlantic slave route
Africa to the Caribbean
finally arriving in slave fields
of the American South.

Plants and animals from the motherland
arrived with us on slave ships
only animals were treated better
cared for more
plants were watered and sunned
we were below, chained in darkness
hungry and thirsty
okra, watermelon, sesame and rice
travelled with us
to adapt, then grow and thrive
inside new soil.

In America, we name our cuisine
soul food
binding our motherland
to us forever
in the special ways
we plant, harvest and slow cook
seasonal fruits, vegetables, and meats
in a strange land
to honor and remember all whom
we love when we were free
in our homeland.

Soul food softens
the bitter roots of slavery
tangible evidence
of spiritual and sensory
connections
to the vastness of West Africa
through many people groups
where we were gathered
and stolen away
we eat to remember
to never forget our origins.

SLEEP I AM FREE

When I sleep, I dream I am bending down in our family's fields
Planting seeds inside dark, rich, fragrant soil that tingles my nose
Watching the sun and rain caress and bless the seeds
As I pray over them to grow into enough food for our village.

When I sleep, I dream that I am farming again in our family's fields
Land that we have tilled over generations
My hands pulling up and out all that chokes crops
Seeing stalks grow tall and seeing vines grow greener curls.

When I sleep, I dream I am harvesting in our family's fields
Gathering ripe fruit and full-grown vegetables
So much, heavy bounty my arms hurt carrying these earthen gifts
Smiling because we have food for winter.

sesame,
beans,
nuts,
cashews,
groundnuts,
cassava,
cocoa,
millet,
melons,
rice
palm kernels,
sorghum,
bananas
plantains
yams

When I sleep, I dream there is enough from our family's fields to cook moi moi, jollof rice, peanut stew, roasted plantains, with fufu. My famer's hands harvest enough to last the winter with evidence of plenty from our family's fields.

Moi moi is steamed black-eyed pea pudding. Jollof rice is rice seasoned with African spices and cooked with tomatoes. Every community has its own version.

A BOWL FULL OF MY PAST

everything looks strange, feels strange, is strange
after such a long, long time tossing
churning tight inside heavy, cold chains
our skins are split and gone gray like cold ashes
insides of stomachs and release of bowels
cover all of us with filth
why can't i die when so many others have been thrown
overboard. dead i can fly back home to my people.
dead i can be free. instead i still feel. i am alive
in a body that refuses the command of my mind
to let go, separate and be at peace.

everything is worse on legs that no longer hold me up
i feel the crack of a whip opening my back
more blood does not change that i can't stand straight
like a full grown man anymore
the sunlight hurts, the fresh air bites oozing wounds and my ears
cannot hear what is said out of the ghost mouths
my eyes roll back and i wait for death to come and take me
but sleep comes instead and i collapse as night falls
my nose wakes me with the smell of home
i must be dreaming home again but the smell of peas and okra
stay with me waking me up to memories

planting in the earth, watering the crops, harvesting
enjoying the smells of the cooking pot at evening time
rice, peas and okra the best food in life
my eyes open to the dream, only to see an elder woman
stirring a cooking pot with a large wooden spoon
when she sees my eyes are staring with disbelief
she speaks to me in my language and says
here is our food to give you comfort, to make you alive again.
I say *mother i don't want to live* but in my heart, i long
for what is lost to me and move the chains to take and eat
a bowl full of my past.

THIS STRANGE LAND

Where have we landed? Where are we now?
Sun is not sun of my village.
Our land is neither flat nor straight
against the horizon
but some dry, some wet, some thick with jungle
all fertile.

We took shade under trees nappy like my hair
fruit lush and plentiful our dark ground welcome seed
to grow melons, sesame, beans, kola nuts,
cassava, cocoa, rice, palm kernels
and so many kinds of bananas.

Herded together from below these ships
chained into the market to be sold to ghost people
in an unknown land where nothing
welcomes me or my eyes
we are confused and shocked
at the fast changes.

My head hurts with thoughts that smash
I see those in chains like me
I hear languages that are one word the same
many other words so different
we are alike in our terror, we feel the same pain
Oh, Creator help us to live in this strange land.

Kola nuts refers to the seeds from trees native to the tropical rainforests of Africa.

AFRICA TO AMERICA

We planted, harvested and ate
Corn
Rice
Peanuts
Dried beans
And yams.

In America
We planted corn
Raised rice in wet fields
Harvested peanuts
Picked and dried beans
Didn't find yams
So we ate sweet potatoes.

In Africa
In America
It is the same okra and greens
Gave us strength
Made our skins shine
Kept our heads on
Food gave us hope.

DARK FOOD FOR DARK PEOPLE

Their food is like the *buckra*
White, plain, bland, unflavored
Sugared inviting fat.

African pepper is *Mpua uzia*
From the *uziza* plant
Hot, peppery to keep fat away.

Negro pepper for Negro people
Roasted, smoked, great
In pepper soup for pregnant women.

Our food is like us Africans
Colored, spicey, peppery
To spark life, not imitate death.

Buckra is a West African word for Whites.

CARIBBEAN CUISINE

Ehuru, calabash nutmeg
AKA Jamaican nutmeg
Roasted to release unique flavors.
Caribbean like the people
Special, piquant and sweet
Like *jerk* seasoning
Roasted by enslavement and colonialism
Caribbeans fought for a freedom
Translated into a food the world
Has never known or savored.

Jerk is a style of cooking native to Jamaica in which meat is dry rubbed or wet marinated with a tangy spice mixture called Jamaican Jerk Spice.

TOMATOES IN SLAVE TIMES

The rich color deepens
Darkens as the sun warms it
Tightening the skin
Until I bite through fragile soft
Seeds, pulp and juice
Burst in my mouth
Two or three scented tomatoes fill the belly
Chase away constant hunger
I pick three for master
One for the slave.

Cooked, red thickens our stews
We eat it ripe and unripe
They grow in many different colors
All kinds of different shapes
Baked or roasted in hot coals
Changes the outside feel
Grilled outdoors or pickled in jars
Changes the flavors
We even dried them to eat on long trips.

After the chance to slip them
Into deep pockets or under your shirt
Pushing hunger back
Often times we pick them green
Slice and coat with corn meal
Frying in a little grease until hard and crispy
When there is wood for the fire
Lard enough to share
Time for frying.

Tomatoes remind me of slave life
Left alone we grow juicy
Their vines produce again and again
Til they bend with ripen fruit
Yet skin cracks from too much sun
Wild or cultivated
Fruit or vegetable
Tart or sweet
Don't make a whole meal, just good side eatin.

WATERMELON SONGS

Not easy to grow
The finest watermelons
The right amount of
Sandy soil
Lots of burning sun
Huge amounts of water
Space for the vines to run.

Red, yellow, orange even white
Meat inside, there are over 1000
Kinds of melon
Domesticated in Africa
Grown all over the world
Summer sings
Sweet watermelon songs.

OUR FOOD

Food
Connects us thru time
Across geography
Tells our personal and collective stories.

Food
Covers us thru struggles
Across generations
Manifests in our cooking.

Food
Creates us thru tastes
Across Africa and the Diaspora
Our culture evolves.

FROM THE FIELDS AND WATERS

Darkest people from wide fields
And salty waters
Gave the world better agriculture
Because land, sea and oceans
Are our partners we wrestled
Subdued to sustain our lives for generations.
We never envisioned
That these abilities would cause other nations
To capture our children and force them
Into agricultural slavery
To cultivate their crops, increase their riches
Darkest people for hundreds of years
Killed far away from Mama Africa.

THE WHOLE TRUTH

Uncovering the truth of Africa's history
Cultures and foods
Freeing us from European prejudices
Turned into racists systems
Designed to justify slavery, colonialism
And normalize bigotry
Denying the beginning of us as humans
On the African continent
Originators, Innovators and the first people
Who flavored the world.

AFRICAN TO AFRICAN AMERICAN CUISINE

Fufu became cornbread
Moi moi stayed black-eyed peas
With a piece of pork to flavor
Peanut stew remained peanut stew.

Yams became sweet potatoes
Greens stayed greens
With a piece of pork to flavor
Rice remained rice yet different kinds.

Coffee remained a familiar taste
With okra creating gumbo, jambalaya,
Pepperpot, rice and peas while introducing
Frying fish and BBQ meats.

Fufu: pounded yams that serves as bread. Moi moi: steamed black-eye pudding. Gumbo and Jambalaya are Creole and Cajun rice dishes of French, African and Spanish influence. Pepperpot is a thick stew made in West African and the Caribbean before being brought to Philadelphia and sold by Colonial Black women in the 19th century. Rice and Peas is an African, Jamaican and African American dish.

SLAVERY: COOKING WITH LITTLE TO MAKE TASTY

DISTRIBUTION OF SLAVES IN U.S. 1860

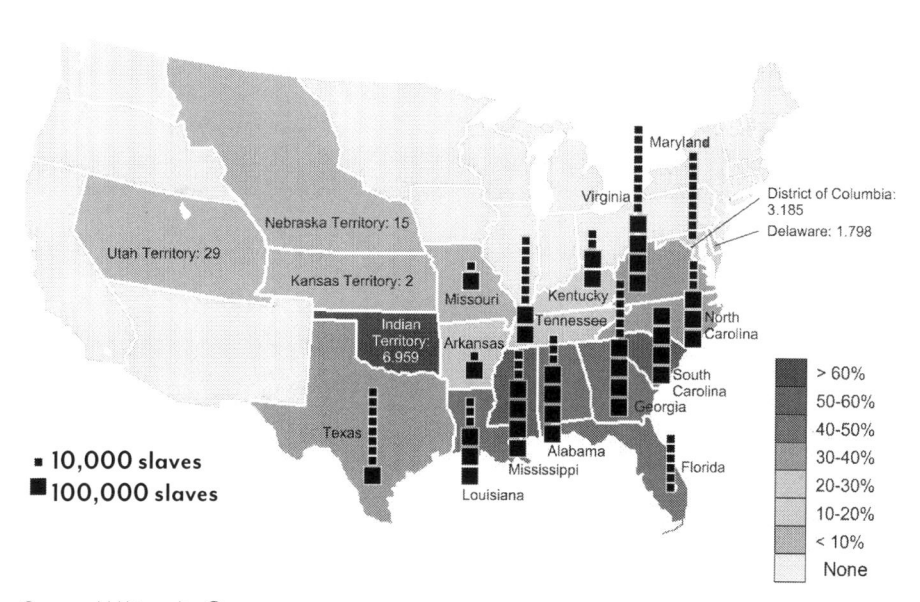

Source: Wikimedia Commons

FOOD AND FREEDOM

Food and freedom are combined
To tell the truth about the African
In America.

How food was our first refusal
Against slavery
In America.

We refused to eat when captured
Early resistance
Before America.

They broke our teeth
And clenched jaws
On the way to America.

They fed us slabber
White flour, grease and spice
On the ship to America.

Some decided to die
Others decided to live
In America.

Food and freedom are combined
To tell our stories about the Africans
In America.

WAR AND FAMINE IN THE NEW WORLD

On the journey to the new world
We didn't lose all we treasure
We kept our dignity
Love for family
Determination to be free
Kept the old ways, our values
Remembered the tastes of long ago memories.

On the journey to the new world
We lost nothing of real value
We kept every important thing
Inside our hearts
Culture was carried in our bones
Our ancient traditions
Inspired us to live despite enslavement.

On the journey to the new world
We lost none of our choices
Some decided life was better
In the spirit world
Others decided slavery would not kill them
They would endure this trouble
Like so many famines and wars.

ENTERING THE NEW WORLD

Sullivan's Island
First sight and first stop
To enter Charleston
Where most came to slavery
The coastline looked similar
To Africa
What cruelty this new place
Was not home.

Carolina gold rice
No one could farm rice
Until Africans worked the land
This is the rice
Important to world commerce
Slavery ended
Free labor ended
Carolina rice was no longer cultivated.

Monetized what was not white
This rice is because of slavery
The cost to produce it came
With the sweaty deaths of Black people
That built Charleston
Made the White folks super rich
Made the Black folks super poor
Few preserve the true story.

ANOTHER DAY A SLAVE

Slavery shadows
Limited lives
Ruins from overwork
Never blessed to live long enough.

That death dog that bit Elder Brotha
Is chasing all of us too
Makes me give massive thanks
Each day I wake.

Having a portion of a mind
Still alive inside of a body
I greet the sun with thanks to God
Have Mercy!

GOD WILL CALL US BY OUR REAL NAMES

Male, 38
Male, 22
Male, 16
Male, 31
Male, 5
Female, 28
Female, 14,
Female, 16
Female, 8
Male, 41
Male, 18
Male, 35
Male, 2
Female, 3
Female, 27
Male, 25
Male, 20
Female, 42
Female, 12
Male twins, 4
Baby

Massa owned 22 of us-es
Never call us-es by right names
Point, call out, yell

Old Nigger
Bowlegged Boy
Bighead Boy
African Nigger
Young Nigger
Red bone Nigger
Black Nigger
Yella Nigger
Ginger Nigger
Greeneyed Nigger

Blue Nigga
Crippled Nigga
Blackie
Yella boy
Heifa
Dark boy
Lil nigga
Mammy
Niggagal
Twin Picaninnies
NiggaBaby
N when he happy
Auntie or Uncle

Even when massa count
N mark us-es in his book
Never call us-es by real names
We are numbers
By the seasons us-es live

African names like tribes
Be beat outta us-es, meanings long forgot
We name us-es
Call the names
We choose in secret

Answer to whatever *toubob* say
Answer quick or the whip fly
But we know who us-es is
God knows us-es by true names.

When us-es die
N go straight to heaven
Past the pain of slavin on earth
God will call our names,
Real secret, African names.

Ekene, 38, Praise
Akachi, 22 The hand of God
Chukulakamiji,16, I walk with God
Obi, 31, Heart
Amadi, 5, Free born
Abimbola, 28, Born into wealth
Akin, 14, The heroic one
Mofeoluwa, 16, I love God
Diglola, 8, Abundance
Abiola, 41, born in honor
Eniola, 18, a person of wealth
Ifeolowa, 35, God's love
Chinge, 2, May God not forget me
Nduka, 3, Life is more important
Eba, 27, Understanding
Azubuike, 25, Strength gathered from past experience
Freeman, 20, a free man
Abeni, 42, We asked for her and we have her
Ebony, 12, Black or dark brown
Juba and Juma, 4, Dance and born on a Friday
Kamau, baby, Quiet warrior

And we will answer God
with our real names.

Toubob: Central and West African word for Whites.

The word "nigger/nigga" is used in this poem for historical accuracy and because of the violence of the word to dehumanize and de-identify my ancestors who were collectively honorable and brave even during enslavement.

MASTERS ARE

Mostly cruel
Cruel
Somewhat cruel
Each of my masters is
Cruel to me.

I watched a trapped fox
Chew off its leg
To escape to freedom
I want to be free
Even more.

Slavery is no good
For any person
I am not an animal
No matter what
Masters insist.

Third generation
Enslaved
My masters say
He a happy slave.

POOR PICANNINY GAL

Efua is with child again.
I am the midwife that helped her ma
birth her and it was on a Friday.
Her name had to be Efua
girl child born on a Friday
though slaves call her Effie
and the masters call her Sue.

Efua, her love name
gives her identity and purpose
connects her to all who went before
so she will remember she is more
than a slave.
We call her Efua in secret
only in the slave quarters.

Efua will birth her fourth child.
She is a child herself at 14 seasons.
Master won't leave her alone.
Her babies are pulled from her breast milk
as soon as they can eat solids.
Sold away but not before she names them
whispers their love names inside their ears.

Her body is tired from no rest
between births and chopping cotton.
I feed her tomatoes, boiled nettles
to make her baby grow strong.
Efua ask "why save my baby to be a slave"
I say "we are a people of life, not death.
The baby must not die inside you."

Efua is with child again.
I am the midwife that helps birth her babies
The only one present to hear her name them
based on the day they are born.
This is the one gift of freedom she can give
One child to another
One slave to another.

KAMAU DIES IN THE COTTON PATCH

Stunned my mind pauses
Grief begins to fill up all the empty spaces
He is too young to fall down dead
But that is what happened.

Shocked my mind stops
Mourning bursts like a tight pig's bladder
Spilling bits and pieces everywhere
I never think he die so young.

Picaninnies never have good food
Never regular or enough
We grown folks give them what we can
But they sickly from birth.

Poor mother, poor father
How you get over losing your sweet child
Burying the who you birthed, missing the child
You should never outlive.

Now we are forced to say
Remember the rainy season
When Kamau died a *knee baby*, we don't know why
Working in the cotton fields, he fell down dead.

Knee baby: Southern expression for the child that stands at the parent's knee and that precedes the baby in the arms.

HOW TO TELL A SLAVER

How to tell a plant from a weed
A friend from an enemy
An abolitionist from a slaver?

Plants and weeds are both green.
Enemies pretend to be friends but friends don't.
Abolitionists and slaver can both be White.

Plants produce fruits and vegetables.
Friends love and not hate.
Slavers destroy not save, protect or help.

When you work the land
You learn plants from weeds.
Seasons teach you seed, soil, planting, and harvest.

Friends provide richness in life
Comfort, understanding, laughs
Like family they give life true meaning.

Slavers give excuses for forgetting
We folks too when they make us
Work the jobs they hate.

Weeds get pulled so they don't choke
Plants. Their actions are the difference
Between friend and foe, abolitionist and slaver.

FREEDOM IS FOOD

Early 1800's escapes begun first
By Black Abolitionists
Travel quickly silently at night
Follow the North Star

The journey North
Hundreds of miles
Underground Railroad
Is one way to freedom.

Sometimes food grabbed
To carry, other times ate
What we could find on the way
Freedom fed our bellies.

How many escaped
On the *Underground Railroad*
No one knows
Thousands ran to freedom.

How many safe houses,
Hidden, secret rooms
Tight spaces underground
Squeeze in to hide from slavers.

Some who helped
Others who hurt
But freedom is a fiery hunger
That never dies.

The Underground Railroad was a network of people (African Americans, Native Americans and Whites) offering shelter and aid to escaping enslaved people from the South.

CORN AND PORK

Master think Master better than slave
Better man
Better thoughts
Better husband
Better father
Well he eat corn and pork
Slave eat corn and pork too.

Master not better than slave
Not better man
Not better thoughts
Not better husband
Not better father
His corn has eggs and better pork pieces.
Mine is *mush* and *chitlins*.

Master and slave are kin folks
Wrong to own another
Wrong to enslave
Wrong to hurt our women
Wrong to starve our children
We raise his corn and his pigs
We cook his corn and fry his pork.

Master not better than slave
We eat yam and greens
With our corn and pork
We grow our gardens
Hunt and fish
To grow strong enough to keep on
Living.

Mush is cornmeal porridge or pudding. Chitlins (Chitterlings) the small intestines of pigs, although sometimes they can be intestines from other animals.

PORKY PIG

Tribute to the lowly pig
Southern hero
Even the smallest pig pieces
Made tasty by slaves.

We baked the ham
But ate the feet
We BBQed the ribs
But ate the *jowl*.

We fried the bacon
But ate snout, tail
And turned intestines
Into tongue slappin chitlins.

Tribute to the germy pig
Confederate mascot
We eat littlest pig pieces
Deciding to live.

Jowl is inexpensive meat that comes uncut on the "rind" and lends flavor to beans, peas, and greens.

ROASTIN RABBIT

I trap it
I skin it
I season it
I cook it
Until it done.

Ain't no secret
To roastin rabbit
To fill an always
Hungry Slave
Belly.

A FEW SPECIAL MEALS

Few happy times
We ate pepper rabbits
Hominy and okra soup.

Pa hunted rabbits
Adding peppers
To be shared with many.

Ma fixed a pot of hominy
With steady stirring
A bigger pot of okra soup

Simmered with smells
Inviting everyone to bring
Their bowl for a taste.

ANOTHER HERCULES IN VIRGINIA

This Hercules was both the slave property
And outstanding cook of George Washington.

There is no drawing that remains of him
Yet his cooking, his recipes live on

Claimed by Martha Washington. An early celebrity
He was one of the most famous chefs

In his time for doing English style food.
The legacy of a Black man as a Black Chef

Impacting the food that all Americans eat
But not receiving any credit

GIVEN TO GEORGE WASHINGTON, 1767

He was a Hercules in the kitchen
Subduing slavery with his pots and pans clanging
From his stirring magic

Creating miracles from fruits and vegetables
At a time when Black was despised
When the cotton and tobacco fields required
His sweat

He was a Hercules in the kitchen
Destroying the monsters of racism with hands
That cooked, baked and served

Dishes that had never been known or tasted
Spices and herbs combining
American and African tastes
For a new southern cuisine

George Washington took his freedom
His wife Martha took his recipes
She who never entered a kitchen

He was a Hercules in the kitchen
Who ran away up North
Escaping chains on his body and mind
Better a life of hidden freedom

Than a slave in the kitchen of a president
He was a Hercules in the kitchen
Who cooked delicious for himself.

GEORGE WASHINGTON, SLAVEHOLDER

Undo the honest, kind myth
Of President George Washington

George Washington was easily angered
A slave holder and ignorant man

Hercules Posey a slave worked
His way up from the fields to the kitchen

Cooked meals that the Washingtons
Loved and admired

So George took him to Philadelphia
To never be without his good food

Every six months Hercules Posey was returned
To Virginia to keep his enslavement intact

He could never buy his freedom, his wife
Or his children but a son Richard could learn to cook

Hercules Posey was sent to the fields
Lest he become uppity and forget his slave place

He ran to freedom from Virginia
President George Washington was angry

Wrote to slavers "find him and return him to slavery"
Wrote "Hercules Posey was privileged"

Asked "Why would Hercules want to be free"
Not slaving for me, the President of the United States.

Historians don't repeat the myth of the cherry tree
Tell the truth about a terrible slave holder.

ANOTHER HEMINGS IN VIRGINIA

This Hemings was both the slave property
And outstanding cook of Thomas Jefferson.

There is no portrait that remains of him
Yet his cooking, his recipes live on hidden

By time and history. An early celebrity
Chef James, he was one of the most famous

In his time for doing French style food like
The Snow Egg.

Thomas Jefferson enslaved 607 people with
400 on his Monticello plantation.

He gave small rations to the enslaved so they
Gardened to live.

From this plantation, James Hemings goes to France
To learn French cuisine.

He trained his brother to cook French fries, ice cream
And macaroni pie. Peter became the Slave Chef

When James purchased his freedom, yet dying young
With his recipes cooking in his head.

The Snow Egg is a meringue dessert.

CHEF JAMES HEMINGS

James Hemings saw too much, felt too much
Son of a white slaver owner and the black woman he owned
Eldest son watched Thomas Jefferson repeat the rape
On his younger sister while she bore his children

James Hemings was the first to be trained, as a chef in France
It is a mockery to say the first American cause
No one, especially Jefferson, saw him as human
Hemings took lessons to learn how to speak fluent French

James Hemings returned to America to be with family
Jefferson pondered how best to keep them all enslaved
His conscience soothed because he paid Hemings wages
Even as President, he was in debt most of his life

James Hemings purchased his freedom in exchange
For his brother's enslavement to the kitchen
His freedom without family was lonely and empty
He killed himself at 36. French cooking was not enough.

IGBO LANDING

Is where proud *Igbo*
Decided never to be
Slaves
And walked into the water
Until they were free.

I honor those
Who said freedom or death
No slavery
For us or our generations
They are free
Forever.

I honor those
Who said freedom and life
Yes to slavery
For us but not for our generations
Who will be free some day
But we will live now.

Igbo landing
Is where my ancestors
Made life and death choices
The choice for life
Means I am here
To write this poem.

Igbo means a people of southeastern Nigeria and their language.

SOUL FOOD: AFRICA TO AMERICA

THE TRIANGULAR TRADE ROUTE

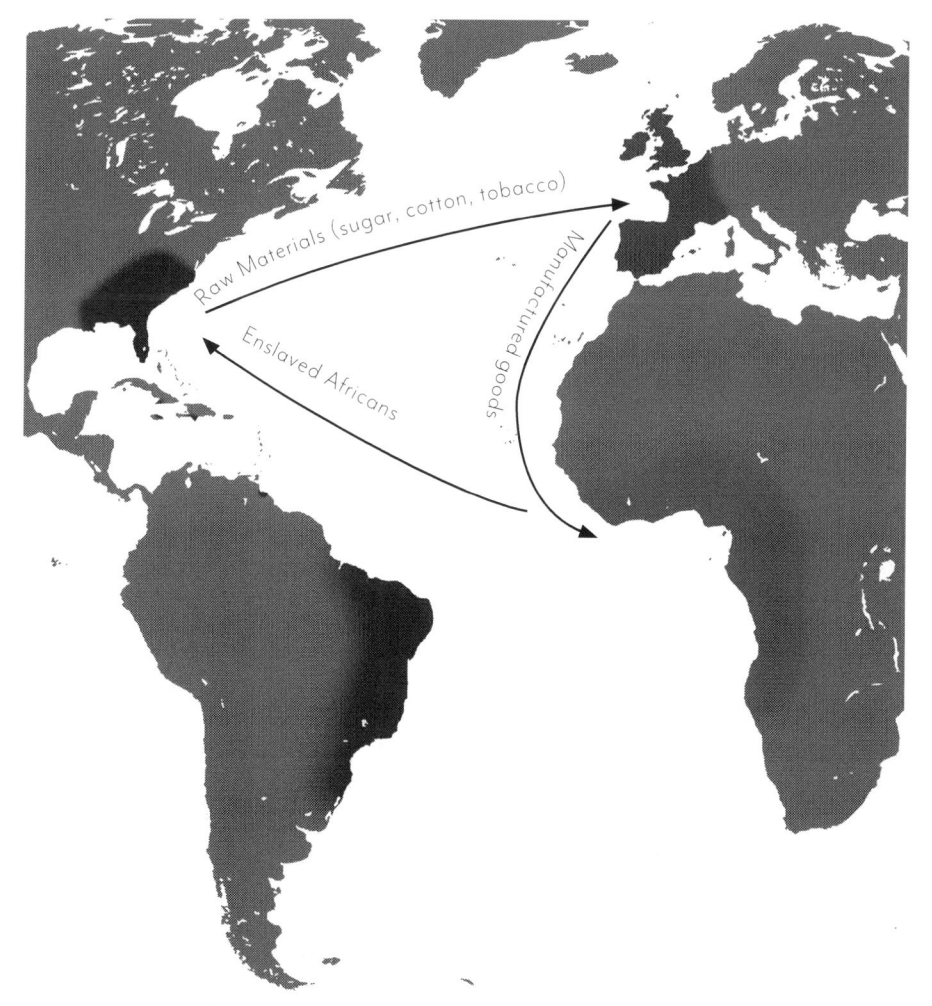

Raw Materials (sugar, cotton, tobacco)

Manufactured goods

Enslaved Africans

Source: Wikimedia Commons

GOD, LOVE AND SOUL FOOD

Like God and like love
We named soul food
For the spiritual connections
To both God and love.

Soul food testifies to all
What is most important
Our God, Our love and
Our food.

We can feel the good food
Going into our souls
Honoring what it sustains in us
God, love and food.

THE BLUES IN FOOD

Boom Boom Boom Boom
Bang Bang Bang Bang
Boom Boom Boom Boom
Haw Haw Haw Haw

The Blues rhythm shows up
In food too.
My mind follows the cadence
My mouth tastes bittersweet rhythms.

BLACK IRON SKILLETS

Families oldest, blackest
Cast iron skillets
Leftover fried love
Fired deeply black inside
Generations of women frying soul food.

One skillet is for fish, nothing else.
One skillet is for chicken,
And the last one is for pork chops.
No oils are mixed, no meats are
Exchanged.

Black women stay serious bout
Frying, food and Jesus.
Don't mess with either or neither.
They clean their cast iron skillets
Right and burn them blacker.

GREASE ADDICTION

It is real addiction
To crave fried

Fried meats, fish, potatoes
Fatty taste of heated oil

Lard, vegetable, canola
Loving that grease

Even saving it used
To add more crisped flavor.

It is true addiction
To insist on charred

Browned, blackened
Flash, pan or deep fried

Knowing the exact sizzle
sound means its crispy done.

Tasting that crackling
In your mouth from char.

It is cultural addiction
When food must be scorched

Burnt, or red-hot crisped
Heated, oil slick before it satisfies.

CHOW CHOW

Harvest what is left in the garden
Fat cucumbers
Bumpy cauliflowers
Deep green cabbage leaves
Cabbages formed and unformed.

Include your favs from the garden
Sturdy bell peppers
Red, green and yellow
Dice onions with diced tomatoes
Red and Green

Don't forget fresh red cayenne
Peppers or dried peppers
Salt to taste
Chopping cabbage smaller
Into bite-sized pieces

Pickling and canning salt
Mix well
Overnight then chill
In clean canning jars
Rinse completely

Get your southern spices added
Celery seed or not
Mustard seed or not
Dry mustard or not
Turmeric or not

Ginger or not
Ground cinnamon or not
Ground cloves or not
Crushed pepper flakes or not
White vinegar with
White sugar

Mix your spices completely
Into the chopped vegetables
Before placing in canning jars
Seal and boil in a water bath.

Sweet Chow Chow
Hot Chow Chow
Mild Chow Chow
All are delicious Chow Chow.

WE COOK WITH LITTLE TO FEED MANY

Take one piece of meat
The one piece you can afford
Ham hock, fat back, turkey neck
Throw into water or broth
With favorite spices
Cut up onions, a dried red pepper and boil
Until flavor fills the pot and the smell
Fills the home

Add your washed and picked greens,
Turnips, mustards, collards or a mixture
Your peas with bad ones thrown out
Beans washed and plumped back up
And boil
Slow cooking at its best
To feed large numbers of family, friends
Visitors who drop in welcomed to the pot

Each family boils for a specific time
Crunchy that has a bit of fight left
Smooth that is boiled until soft as butter
Sliding down throats
Shared processes of cooking
Generations of Black hands prepare
Memories that we eat
With hot sauce, vinegar and Chow Chow.

HEAD HASH

Boil the hog head
It its own broth
Cut up every part
Inferior and otherwise
Cut up the boiled hog head.

Make hog head hash
Chopped up small
Tongue, eyes, tender meat
Simmer for 30 minutes
Mixed with BBQ sauce.

In slavery, reconstruction, segregation
Eating to defy hunger
Eating to survive and thrive
Wasting absolutely nothing.

A TALL SLIM BOTTLE OF HOT SAUCE

Hot, hot Sauce
Chili peppers
Spicy condiment
Sharp seasonings

Lover of fried catfish
Necessary to finish
All of our food
Fish, fowl and vegetables

Splashes of ripe red liquid
Right amount of tang
If it is missing from the table
Run from the food.

DANDELION GREENS

Sustainability in the earth
Good medicine
Golden blossom tops
Roots to leaves
Considered a weed by ignorants
This plant heals
Abundance of protein
Iron and helps you pee
Dandelion greens protects
Against disease and boosts
Good health.
Dandelion greens
Ancient friend to African
Slaves
Growing wild, easy to pick
Boil and share.

THE MAJESTY OF GREENS

Leafy dark green collards grow
And grow
Sharp tangy wavy mustards row
After row
While turnips hide beneath the soil
Two offerings from one seed.

Mixing the three is soul food
At its best
Collards don't boil away like the rest
Mustards adding peppery spice
Turnips offering both ends of savory
A *mess* of tasty greens.

Mess of greens is a Southern expression for an unmeasurable amount of greens.

GREEN EXPERTS

Mustards are picked by hand
Cook away quickly
Dense and tangy.

Collards are cut into bite sizes
Leaves more smooth greens
Left to boil in the pot.

Some greens experts cook both
Together, smooth with a little tang tang
Good greens eatin.

Some greens experts start with bacon,
Add onion and chicken stock
Tasty greens eatin.

Some greens experts start with fatback
Add dried red peppers, water to cover
Spicy greens eatin.

Some greens experts start with ham hocks
Add a little vinegar, a little water
Deep South greens eatin.

Other greens experts use smoked turkey
Add fresh garlic to taste
Non-pork greens eatin.

Other greens experts use chopped onions
Add smoke seasoning
Vegan greens eatin.

Other greens experts sauté theirs
Add powered garlic and onion
Quick greens eatin.

Other greens experts fight bitterness
Add a pinch of white or brown sugar, honey dab
Sweet greens eatin.

Mustards can be eaten raw
Cut up into salads
Collards stems flavor soups

And green smoothies
Greens, our adopted traditional food.

POTLIKKER

Pot liquid
Green juices
Brothy water
Packed with goodness
And healthy too.

Growing up
Southern style
Potlikker from greens
Went into my bottle
As a brown baby.

Potlikker into soup
With vegetables.
Reduced with onions,
Tomatoes and spices
To make a sauce.

Bottom leavings
In greens pot
Delicious potlikker
Pork pieces with corn pone
Crumbled or dunked.

Corn Pone: a type of southern bread using corn meal, water and salt.

TURNIP GREENS AND BLACK APPETITES

Turnip greens are bitter
With stickers
To try to protect them
From Black appetites.

Lil sugar beats the beast
Down and releases
Tangy sweet tastes
For Black appetites.

Cut turnip roots on top
Squared and simmering
Until a well done crunch
Satisfies Black appetites.

A MARRIAGE OF LOVE

Black eyed peas married
Buttermilk cornbread
Because he was crispy hot
To her soft mash.

Black eyed peas vowed
Never to be
Peas alone on a plate
Without cornbread.

Cornbread agreed though
It could go alone
It tasted sweeter when the two
Were together as one.

FOR CAROLINA RICE

Growing rice
For hundreds of years
In Africa.

Rice plantations
Required the removement of trees
In South Carolina.

Free labor of thousands of slaves
Worked to death
In America.

A BRIEF HISTORY OF RICE

Jollof Rice
Broken Once

Red Rice
Broken Twice

Rice, Rice
Made South Carolina

Rice, Rice
Took Slaves Lives

100 million pounds
Made Rice King

Jollof Rice: rice seasoned with African Spices and cooked with tomatoes. Red rice: a classic Low country side dish that is made by cooking with long grain white rice, bacon, onions, garlic and tomato paste with antioxidants, vitamins and minerals.

HOPPIN JOHN AKA BLACK-EYED PEAS

Black-eyed peas
Bi-racial
Combining colors

Mixed
Light brown to beige
With a touch of black

Small to large
Eye color from black to brown
Red and pink too

It is an eye
That sees the scope
Of Black history

All start green
Like the cowpea from Africa
Then dry into brown.

It has a cousin
Purple hull pea
Green with a pink spot.

Colorful legumes
Cooked into Hoppin John
Rice and peas.

THE BEGINNING OF US

Yams
Huge

Yams
Hairy

Yams
Healthy

Yams
Tubers

Yams
Twins

African yams
Transform

to sweet potatoes
cause we long for yams.

OKRA STORIES

Okra
Gumbo

Original
African

Transported
USA

Thickner
Accompanies

Greens
Peas

Beans
Rice.

HOW TO EAT WATERMELON

Cold or natural
Watermelon connoisseurs eat the heart
That sweetest, firmest, reddest
Center circle

Some say eat the red meat
Others eat til red turns pink
Others eat down to the white rind
Sweet and bitter mixed

Have the right mind when eating
Watermelon
You are eating Africa and all
Stored memoires that come with tasting

Your cells respond to juciness
From centuries of domesticating melons
Digesting power that strengthens
Black bodies

Eat watermelon with gratitude
Understanding its role in keeping us alive
During slavery
It blesses from the rind to the fruit.

WATERMELON LYRICS

Watermelon
Watermelon
Good to the rind
Makes my heart
Go flippty fine.

Watermelon and Black folks.
How the Whites make fun of us
Caricatures of Black folks eating
Garden fresh watermelons
Making fun of Blacks and melons.

Wise Black folks knew melons
Kept us alive in the hot, slave fields
Mostly water, they kept us from fainting
Full of vitamins, they kept us healthy
Deep red reduces inflammation to prevent disease.

Black folks and watermelons
Are a great partnership to keep a race alive
Even the rinds helps prevent sunburn
Smeared across the skin.
We pickled the rind and ate it too.

Watermelon rhyme is what I grew up hearing from local watermelon vendors.

MY HEALING GARDEN: COMO TO LIMURU TO MADISON

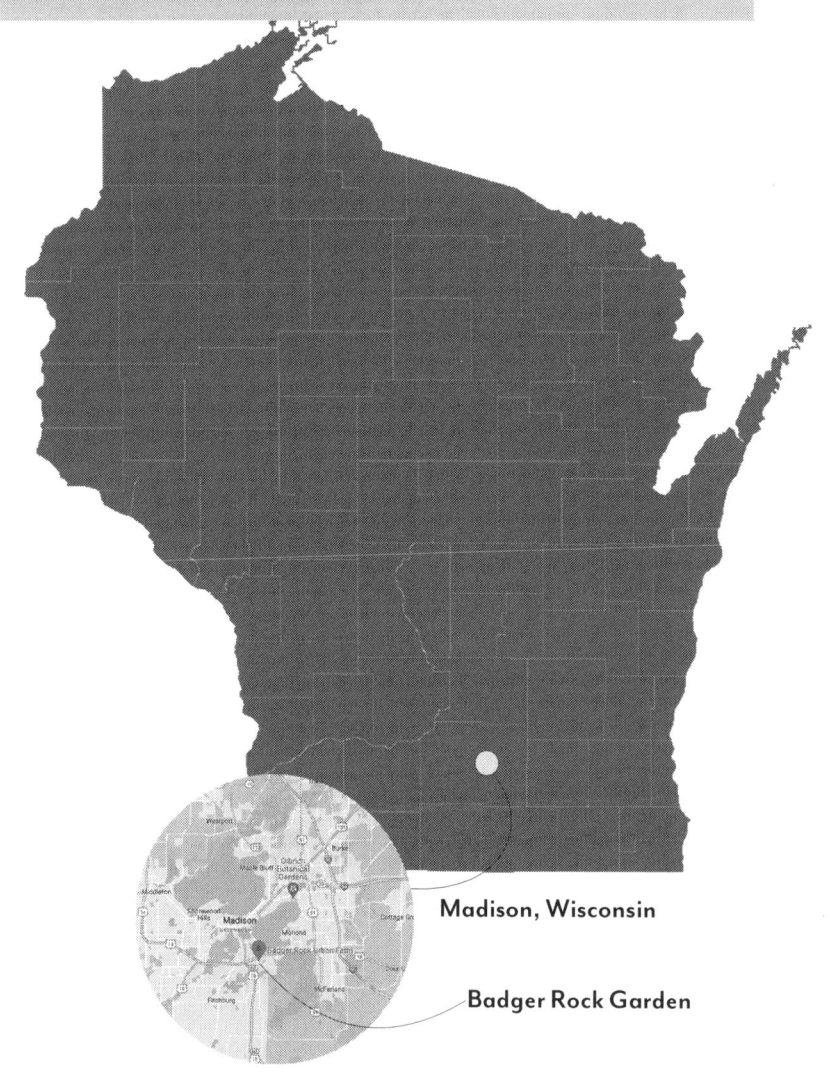

Madison, Wisconsin

Badger Rock Garden

LAND ACKNOWLEDGEMENT

As an African American who lives in Wisconsin, I recognize this land is the ancestral home of the Ho-Chunk Nation, who have called it Teejop (day-JOPE) since time immemorial.

In the first treaty following the Indian Removal Act in 1830, the state government forcibly removed the Ho-Chunk from their home in 1832. In the decades that followed, the federal and state government sought to completely remove the Ho-Chunk from Wisconsin. Despite these attempts, many Ho-Chunk people continued to return to their home in present-day Wisconsin.

I acknowledge the circumstances that led to the forced removal of the Ho-Chunk people, and honor their history of resistance and resilience. The Ho-Chunk Nation and the other ten First Nations residing in the boundaries of present-day Wisconsin remain vibrant and strong.

I recognize and respect the inherent sovereignty of the eleven First Nations that reside in the boundaries of the state of Wisconsin.

— Poet Fabu

GARDENS AND FABU

As a young girl, I walked a rocky, dirt road
In Como, Mississippi
With my Grandma Effie on our way
To her huge garden to pick fresh food
For the family meals.

My small hand in her warm hand
Grandma Effie explained what she planted.
If they were growing good or not.
Why we ate greens, okra, corn, tomatoes, and onions
She also grew sunflowers and gourds to make dippers

As a young adult, I walked a rocky, dirt road
In Limuru, Kenya
With my friend Wanjiku on our way
To extended families' plots to pick fresh food
For the family meals in Nairobi.

With our arms full of produce, she would tell
Me why Kenyans grew white *maize*, not yellow corn
Sukuma wiki, their national greens
Cabbages and beans for their traditional *Githeri*.

As a divorced, single mom
I tried to introduce gardening to my little Woodie
Who is both Kenyan and African American
We started a romaine lettuce and beefsteak tomato garden
In Eagle Heights.

We walked a paved, winding road
Down to the garden area
His small hand in my warm hand
As I explained why we needed to weed and water.

Older, I only ate fresh from summer farmer markets
In Madison, Wisconsin
I went alone, sometimes with friends, to purchase
Seasonally from local farmers
For tasty meals before the hard winters came.

During the COVID Pandemic
I fell critically ill, wondering if I'd ever
Write another poem
A friend asked what I'd like planted in a garden
Released from the hospital, I went to see it.

Collards and cabbages were pushing thru the soil
Tomatoes were scaling wire frames
Along with green peas and cucumbers
I put my hands into the soil and healing began.

Skinny, exhausted, I visited my garden
Several days every week
Pulling weeds, watering and watching new growth
My veggies fed me spiritually and fed me physically
My garden blessed me, returned me to my Grandma Effie's garden.

Como, Mississippi is a small town located 40 miles outside of Memphis, Tennessee. Maize is a Kenyan word for corn. Sukuma wiki is a Kenyan dish made with greens, cooked with onions, tomatoes and Kenyan spices. It is often served and eaten with ugali, a type of maize bread.

THE PATIENCE OF SEEDS

Inside Spring compost
Seeds wait for water and light
Regeneration.

AN ODE TO CUKES

Cucumbers swell
Drinking water into rounded
Seeded rectangles.

HOT PEPPERS

Peppers take their own
Bitter, sharp time to grow
Before they bite your tongue.

GREEN CABBAGE BLUES

Cabbage leaves spread
Wide and wild before curling
From summer heat.

EATING CABBAGE LEAVES

My Mother tended her Mother's garden
With particular fondness
For ginormous cabbage leaves.

I grew up not knowing her love
For cabbage leaves nor even how
they grow wide before curling.

My Aunt told the story of how
Mom would collect cabbage leaves
Cook what others threw away,

Decades later I am growing cabbage
With ginormous leaves
I cook them as greens like Mom.

Cabbage leaves in my mouth
Make me remember Mom
I love tasting what she tasted and loved.

COLLARDS ARE KINGS

Fresh collards are kings
Each leaf rules the garden space
Enormous dark green kingdoms.

SOUL FOOD DIVAS

Eating tops and ends
Above and beneath the soil
Turnip greens are queens.

MUSTARDS

Peppery lime greens
Rumpled tops that grumble
As summer sun heats them.

OKRA BLOOMS

Like a pretty flower
Okra has a beige bloom
Before it elongates
Curves into okra.

It turns purple
Other kinds green in the sun
Varieties from Africa
And America

Mighty okra yearns
To float on top of greens
Until soft and succulent
Pods bursting with flavor.

SOUTHERN OKRA

When you boil it
It is like a southern drawl
Long and soft.

WILD-IN OUT TOMATOES

Tomato plants wild-in out
Growing tall, thick
Fragrant
Unwilling to share space
Tomatoes push away
Every other plant.

Tomato plants heavy
Gathering rounded weight
Green than bright red
Eat them straight from the vine
Warm, juicy
Spice, slice and dip in cornmeal

Fry in hot oil
A meal all on its own
Music inside our bellies
An old southern spiritual
Sung thru fruit/veggie
Wild-in out tomatoes.

BOK CHOY

Newest immigrant
Tasty in soups, stir frys
Greens distant cousin.

AMERICAN PEAS

Spring green pea pods
Tendrils stretching up to climb
Bright sqiggles curl.

LETTUCE PRAISE

Let us praise salads
As the main ingredients
Proving summer's here.

MODERN GARDEN

The rabbits ate my lettuce
Romaine to be specific
I didn't grow it for them
I don't want to share.

The rabbits ate my lettuce
Romaine to be exact
They didn't share it with me
They ate it down to nubs.

The rabbits ate my lettuce
If I had caught them
I would have eaten rabbit stew
With a lettuce salad starter.

BADGER ROCK COMMUNITY GARDEN

Few places in America, in our states,
Cities and communities where people
Are offered raised and container gardens, large beds
Fecund, dark compost to spread
A large variety of seeds and budding plants
Classes to learn gardening techniques
And individual answers to their questions
While maintaining personal dignity with no
Intrusive scrutiny to undermine food justice
Or the purpose of urban agriculture
to feed people well.

At Badger Rock Community Garden
We touch this land and remember Indigenous
Sisters and brothers who farmed first
As we rake compost, select and plant
our cultures thru selections of vegetables.
We greet each other in multiple languages
asking how our gardens are growing
Admiring the beauty of our edibles
Sharing the joy of communal gardening
Smiling and laughing as we work in the hot sun

Dragging the water hose to provide liquid life
For this produce we grow improves our health
And lessens our grocery bills
We are also passionate about the intersection of racial,
Food and environmental fairness
In South Madison, where we struggle against
Food deserts, need affordable family housing
Adequate bus transportation, and to circulate our dollars
within this neighborhood thru jobs and small businesses.
Welcome to the Badger Rock Community Garden
Where people who garden are celebrated.

WHICH KIND OF WATERMELON?

Picnic, Allsweet, Charleston Gray
Crimson Sweet, Icebox, Blacktail Mountain
Bush Sugar Baby, Sweet Beauty, Personal
Golden Midget, Little Darling, Giant
Black Diamond, Yellow Belly, Carolina Cross
Seedless, Big Tasty, Mini Piccolo are just a few
Kinds of watermelons
We know them by striped or green
Seeded or unseeded
Red, orange, or yellow inside.
Watermelons have male and female parts
But the fruit is all juicy, ripen female.

PICKING SWEET MELONS

Thick hard rind
That a finger cannot pierce
Knocking for a sound
That is not hollow
No dents, cuts, bumps
Or lumps
Heavy from being swollen
With water into fruit
Picking the right ripe melon
Is a southern art form
Many claim to know
Most just guess
By the yellow patch
Unless the watermelon man
Plugs it for you
With a nice round circle
That you see and taste.

YOU BETTER GROW

Folks talk to flowers
Do they talk smack to veggies
Threatening them, Grow or else?

NOW WE EAT TO LIVE: LESS FAT, SALT, SUGAR AND RACISM

DISTRIBUTION OF THE 10 LEADING CAUSES OF DEATH AMONG BLACK U.S. RESIDENTS IN 2018

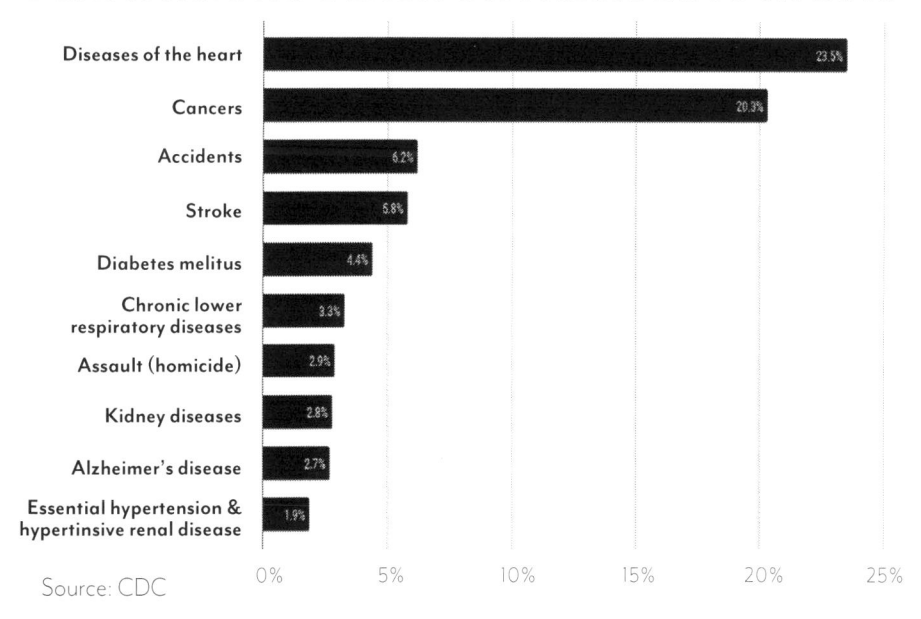

Cause	%
Diseases of the heart	23.5%
Cancers	20.3%
Accidents	6.2%
Stroke	5.8%
Diabetes melitus	4.4%
Chronic lower respiratory diseases	3.3%
Assault (homicide)	2.9%
Kidney diseases	2.8%
Alzheimer's disease	2.7%
Essential hypertension & hypertinsive renal disease	1.9%

Source: CDC

2.9x

Black people are 2.9 times more likely to be killed by police than white people in the U.S. Source: PBS

50%

Half of all police killings are people between 20 and 40 years old.
Source: Statista

CREATOR OF ALL GOOD

We bless you
We thank you
Who feeds us
All that we eat
Makes us strong.

LOOKING BACK ON SLAVERY

we were experts in our language
and literature
we were illiterate in the slavers
communication
so we talked to ourselves and to others
in African languages
in sign languages
with the drums
sometimes no words, just looks
on our face that spoke loud.

we were experts in planting
and harvesting
we knew these crops
though we did not know this land
so we seeded, farmed and harvested
in African ways
in best practices
with passed down
knowledge
that came from several villages
from folks from all over.

looking back on slavery
generations later
we should have been paid
40 acres and a mule
for building this nation with
the sweat
that made European Americans
wealthy and developed this land
40 acres and a mule
was small payment for several
generations of enslaved people.

had our ancestors been compensated
the rich could have said
we paid in full
now we are still owed
for our ancestors' enslavement
we are still owed
because racism never ended
we are still owed
capitalism demands
full payment with interest
we are owed 40 acres and a mule, 21st century value.

BLACK FARMERS TRIBUTE

Deepest joy
To the man and woman
Who touch
Soil with love.

Blessings abound
To the woman and man
Who plant
That we eat well.

Thankfulness
To generational farmers
Who harvest
over seasons and stories.

In 1910 Black Farmers were 14 percent of all farmers with 10 million acres.
In 2017 Black Farmers were 1.4 percent with 5 million acres.

BLACK FARMERS AND NATURE

Earth tells all
Sun too hot
Seeds dry up in heated soil.

Rain overflows
Soaks soil
Seeds float away or clump.

Bugs proliferate
Fruits and veggies
Are ragged holes.

Ahh but Nature happy
Tasty produce
Pretty and plump.

TRIBUTE TO SOUL CHEFS

Soul Food Chefs pour prayers
over the food as
they cook
indigenous plants
locally produced crops
harvested in traditional ways
that sustain the land.

Soul Food Chefs utilize traditions
growing indigenous crops
for food sovereignty
people and communities
to provide cultural food
they grow on their own land.

Soul Food Chefs provide natural foods
for physical and spiritual health
choosing flavors over salt
helping us to live strong
without disease
satisfying us with long life.

DRINKING WELL WATER

When we didn't know better
We drank juice high in sugar, low in fiber
Our favorite flavored powder

When we didn't know better
We drank lemon and sugar
Our favorite Southern lemonade

When we didn't know better
We drank fruit juice with high fructose
Our favorite imitation juices

When we didn't know better
We drank dark and light soda
Our favorite bubbly pops

When we didn't know better
We drank all kinds of beer and
Our favorite weekend liquor

When we did know better
We drank lots of water
Memphis artesian well water.

MISS ANNIE'S TRUE LIFE STORY

The true life story of
My step Great Grandmother
Miss Annie Lockett
Born a slave
Who died a free, rich woman.

In 1865, she was about 13 or 14
When slavery ended
By then she had two of Master's children
Master sold them and she never saw
Her babies again and she never birthed again.

Miss Annie always wanted her back
Scratched cause raised scars itched
Grandchildren didn't like to
Touch the deep scars across her back
From whip lashes.

Beat and whipped so often
A braided pattern could be felt
Thru her clothes
Never asked her bout them lashes
Elders said they were her slave lashes.

Miss Annie was freed
Never stop looking for her lost two
She supported five families on her land
Uncle Lee and Aunt Martha
Aunt Cindy and Uncle Duke.

Uncle Goodman and Aunt Bandy Bug
(Also called Big Momma, but
Her real name was Lenora)
Cousin Jack and Cousin Lucille
And their dozens of children.

Any family member need money
They went to Miss Annie
Miss Annie would give it to them
Or sell a hog or sell a cow
To help family.

Miss Annie's house was the only one
Still on a gravel road
She had peach trees, apple trees,
Pear trees, and plum trees
For her grands and greatgrands' delight.

Miss Annie couldn't read or write
She did recognize her signature X
Her specific drawn X
When folks tried to cheat her
Miss Annie say, "not my X and not my bill."

She married the preacher man,
Her 5th husband when she was a lot older than him
Wavy haired Jim Cunningham was quite the catch
He was my Great Grandfather.

Everyone called him Poppa
He was a good looking widower with grown children
And he died first.
Miss Annie did the impossible
Outlived all five younger husbands.

When she died in 1960 or 1961
She had 189 acres of land in Como, Mississippi.
None of this land remains
It was divided up but nobody felt the same love
For family that she did.

Miss Annie thought she had left all to Big James.
But there was no legal will
My family was her step-children
And she loved them like the lost two.

Miss Annie was an inspiration
More than an American dream
She was the African American reality
Who was over 100 years when she left
For the Glory Land.

Life gave her valleys in her face
Slavery gave her raised mountains
Across her back
She outlived her enemies
And never forgot how to love.

This is authentic Cunningham genealogy.

GRANDMA EFFIE'S LOPSIDED CAKES

Her cakes were lopsided
Plain inside plain outside
A clear glaze
Sugar frosting they called it.

When grandchildren arrived
We'd head to the kitchen
Looking for her leaning cakes
That tasted so good.

Two layers, sometimes three
Can't explain why they were
Always lopsided and leaning
Or so good.

We'd eat up everything
Leaving nothing for the adults
Grandma would say
"Let them eat. Leave those children alone."

We loved our gentle grandma
Who stood between us and our parents
Who always seemed harsher
Ready to correct with spanking.

Grandma was the only parent
Who could rein her daughters in
Protecting her grandchildren
From their sharp words or heavy belts.

Her lopsided sugar cakes
from scratch
Were better than boxed cakes
Bakery cakes or Mama cakes
Plain inside with a clear sugar glaze.

GRANDMA EFFIE'S SCRATCH BISCUITS

I remember Grandma's homemade biscuits
Always from scratch
Mixed and measured in her small hands
Rolled until soft and fluffy.

"How hard is cooking from scratch"
Grandma Effie said
"I watched my mother who watched
Her mother, aunts and women cousins."

Later I did what they did
Changing only a little here and there.
Making food personal
With my own kind of Effie love.

GRANDMA EFFIE'S POKE SALAD

Poke Salad is the same as *Poke Sallet*
First plants to rise up in Spring
Pure poison cooked to perfection
Boil three times
Pouring the water off
The last boil add vinegar.

Grand Daddy Woodie loved *Poke Sallet*
Always eating it with a cut up boiled egg
Hot cornbread, never a biscuit
Good eating, a southern delicacy
Eating in season, never at any other time
Grew wild all over the South.

PINK HAPPY

When i could know her face
as my grandma
and have a child's understanding
of her place in my world
she was a kind, little old lady
with grey tipped hair
pale yellow creased skin
and a voice like a mourning song.

When i could know her ways
as my grandma
and have a child's awareness
of her role in my life
she didn't stay long but died young
her back curved from cotton
fields and her hands crumpled
from planting, weeding and picking.

My grandma liked pink
her youngest daughter told me
i didn't know grandma found a color
she like to see
that she had time for beauty
time to think about and choose
a color to made her happy
that my grandma was young too.

FRIED CORN EXPERT

Every woman in my mom's generation
Had several dishes
cooked expertly.

My mom was a fried southern corn expert
Before GMO corn
just fresh field corn.

Remove green husk and blonde silk
From plump kernels
Cut half on an angle.

Cut the remaining half before scraping
Corn juice
Into a hot cast iron skillet.

Add a little flour, a small amount of grease
Butter and salt for flavor
Then stir constantly

Allow a bit of scorched
Not to burn the corn
But add a smoky taste.

Cook for hours until thickened and dark brown
Her fried corn was artistic expression
From an expert.

GMO: Genetically modified organism is altered corn using genetic engineering techniques which is never the best food for people.

MY DADDY WAS A COOK TOO

Wonderful growing up
With two parents who cooked well.
Mom didn't like cooking. Dad did.

Dad was an Army Sergeant
Who learned by peeling potatoes
But then was excited to cook more.

My parents balanced me
Knowing women didn't have to cook
And men cooked too.

I made my own kitchen decisions
Kicking traditions to the wind
While always able to feed myself.

Staff Sergeant Herman Grant Carter was an awarded career soldier.

GOOD FOOD DURING PREGNANCY

My joy at being pregnant
Caused me to eat
The best farm to table foods.
I ate fresh fish, in season fruits
And organic vegetables
To create a baby who needed my best.

My joy at birthing a son
Caused me to eat
The best low salt, low sugar foods
Since I was breast feeding him.
I ate nothing fried, mostly boiled,
Baked or grilled so that my milk
Would be rich in nutrients.

My joy at having an adult
Who is full of gratitude that nutritious foods
Supported his healthy, strong body
With no medical problems
That he continues to exercise often
And enjoys international foods.

A REAL SOUL FOOD DIET

I'm made of garden collard greens
Crispy hot-water cornbread
Medium size steamed African okra
With cut up onion and red pepper.

I'm made of my mom's scorched fried corn
Cabbage leaves sautéed with smoked pork
Black eyed peas and Chow Chow
The best vegetable plate ever.

I'm made of grilled T-bone steak
Roasted root vegetables
Baked sweet potatoes with a little butter
Sweet seeded Mississippi watermelon.

I'm made of romaine lettuce
Spring mix, red onion, no salt peanuts
Organic ranch dressing mixed with a little
Italian salad dressing.

I'm made of all kinds of beans
Slow cooked with pork or turkey
Cracklin cornbread with fat cracklins
Sweet Southern Lemonade and Ice Tea.

I'm made of soul, love and Black folk's
Cuisine. Organic, fresh, garden grown
Foods overflowing with smells and memories
Of Black family love.

ARRIVING HOME TO DINNER SMELLS

Another hard day of school
Only a few Black kids
At an almost all-white school
Not much that is comfortable
In skin colors, hospitality or
Culture
I race home to stand
At the door of my home
Flavors met me.

My mom's southern scents
One pot slow cooking for hours
Aromas lifting from grandma's
Garden veggies
Grandpa's Mississippi smoked hog
I stand at the door
Use my nose
To tell me what is simmering
In the pot.

Is it ham hocks and pinto beans
Black-eyed peas with fatback
Navy beans and smoked bacon.
Purple hull peas with hog jowls
Red beans over rice
Field peas with neckbones
Butterbeans with hot water cornbread
Great northern beans but turkey necks
Not pork.

Home is my safe place
Smelling favorite meals
As I stand at the door accepting
African American welcome
Through familiar foods that my mom
Cooks for us

Aromatic soul food
Comforting erasure of white racism
From a little Black girl's heart.

MY FAVORITE MEMORIES OF CHILDHOOD DINNERS

Our table is round
With five brown wooden chairs
No cloth padding
We sit down to meals
Say Grace over our food
Then the games begin.

Salad is tough to eat
Mostly we push it around
Around and around on the plate.
When Mom gets tired
Of our playing, the command
EAT rings out.

I'm with my mother, dad
Brother and sister.
I am happy.

Our table is a long rectangle
With more than 20 seats of many
Shapes and colors
We sit down to eat.

Grandpa says a long Grace
Over so much food
While I peek at parents,
Uncles, aunts,
Cousins and grandparents
With their heads bowed.

We are together
Duke the old hound dog farts
Dishes are being passed
Jokes are being told
I am happy.

COMO, MISSISSIPPI MELONS

When my ma was a child
She and her siblings would burst open
Watermelons from their ma's garden
And eat warm, delicious melon
Right in the garden.

When I was a child
Me and my siblings would eat cubed
Refrigerated watermelon
That my ma cut up precisely
Stored in Tupperware.

Both my ma, me and our siblings
Let the watermelon juice
Run down our chins
From stuffing so much into our mouths
Overjoyed as red juice overflowed.

ENJOYING EATING WATERMELON

I eat watermelon
From the red to the white
Eat far past the pink
Almost to the green outside.

I love watermelon
For its natural sweetness
Delicious pulp
Firm tasty insides.

I spit out watermelon
Tiny black seeds
Enjoying them being testimony
Watermelons will continue to propagate.

As a child, I wanted
Watermelon to grow inside
From just one black seed
Then I'd have melon forever.

A MODERN DAY FOOD TRAGEDY REVERSED

As an adult, I realized
I was mostly made of fried foods
Fast food and powered drinks.

Not enough fresh vegetables,
Garden food or
In season fruits.

Once upon a time
I drank various colors
Of dye and sugar.

Strawberry powedered drink,
Grape with a twist of lemon
Nothing but sugar and water.

Once upon a time
I ate boxed foods, can goods
A little frozen but all

Artificial, full of salt.
Artificial, full of potassium.
Artificial, full of phosphorus.

Once upon a time
I became diabetic
Kidney disease was the result.

Now I eat from a garden
Organic and seasonal
I am made from wholesome.

ABOUT THE AUTHOR

Fabu Phillis Carter, is an artist professionally known as Poet Fabu in Madison, Wisconsin. She is a poet, columnist, storyteller and teaching artist who writes to encourage, inspire and remind. Selected as the first African American to become a Madison Poet Laureate (2008–2012), she continues to share the Black experience living in the South, the Midwest and in Africa. She served as poetry editor for Umoja Magazine and Madison Magazine. In 2019, she was poetry editor for the Wisconsin Fellowship of Poets annual edition. She currently serves as poetry editor for the Capitol City Hues and is a culture columnist for the Cap Times newspaper.

Dr. Fabu Carter has a PhD from the University of Nairobi, the African Women's Center. In 2021 she became a Commissioner for the Madison Arts Commission. Also in 2021, she co-hosted Poetry for Life, a telephone poetry session every Thursday with Poet Gary Glazner. In 2022 that changed to an in-person Poetry and Arts Café held on the first Tuesday of each month at the UW South Madison Partnership Office.

Fabu is the author of seven books of poetry, including *Poems, Dreams and Roses* (Madison Arts Commission, 2009), *In Our Own Tongue*, (University of Nairobi Press, 2011), *Journey to Wisconsin: African American Life in Haiku* (Parallel Press, 2011), *Love Poems* (Ironer's Press, 2016). *Journey to Wisconsin* won an Outstanding Achievement in Poetry award from the Wisconsin Library Association. Her last three books are on Mary Lou Williams, jazz genius. They are *Remember Me: Mary Lou Williams in Poetry, Sacred Mary Lou* and *Mary Lou Williams Coloring Book* (all Ironer's Press, 2019, 2020 & 2022). She is a Pushcart nominee in poetry with poems in Rosebud, PMS, Callaloo and the Wisconsin Academy of Science, Arts and Letters. Fabu is launching her newest book, We Eat to Remember: Soul Food Poetry, in 2023. Her website is www.artistfabu.com.

My sincere appreciation to Wendy Vardaman, poet, graphic artist and friend who assisted me in creating this poetry book.

Made in the USA
Middletown, DE
09 April 2025